For my mother and father, who gave me flute lessons
A. P.

For Sarah, Ava, and Molly
M. T.

First edition 2014

Library of Congress Catalog Card Number 2013943992
ISBN 978-0-7636-5856-4

14 15 16 17 18 19 TLF 10 9 8 7 6 5 4 3 2 1

Printed in Dongguan, Guangdong, China

This book was typeset in New Clarendon.
The illustrations were done in watercolor, gouache, ink, and pencil.

Candlewick Press
99 Dover Street
Somerville, Massachusetts 02144

visit us at www.candlewick.com

Jubilee!

One Man's BIG, BOLD, and VERY, VERY LOUD CELEBRATION of PEACE

ALICIA POTTER

illustrated by MATT TAVARES

CANDLEWICK PRESS

As a boy in Ireland, Patrick S. Gilmore loved music. He thrilled to hear the army bands march by.

RUM-TEE-TUM! RUM-TEE-TUM! RUM-TIDDY-TUM-TUM-TUM!

When he was old enough, Patrick joined the town band *and* the choir. He played the flute.

And the cornet.

But what really made his heart sing and his toes tap were many notes. Many, many LOUD notes.

At church, Patrick formed a quartet and arranged all the music. He blended the sounds so beautifully!

Soon Patrick was organizing his own concerts. Every Sunday after church, he and his friends sat on a stone wall and played for anyone who'd listen.

DING DONG!

It was wonderful! But Patrick longed to
hear even *more* notes and even *bigger* sounds.
And he knew just how to accomplish that. He
would become a bandleader!

In 1849, Patrick joined the thousands of people who were leaving Ireland to pursue their dreams in America. Patrick settled in Boston, Massachusetts, which at the time was the country's music capital.

Patrick's dream of becoming a bandleader quickly came true. He led the Charlestown Band, the Suffolk Band, and the Boston Brigade Band. Under his baton, the Salem Brass Band became one of the finest in New England.

Patrick even founded his own ensemble:
the very popular Gilmore's Band.

OM!

But when the Civil War broke out, in 1861, Patrick had battlefields, not bandstands, on his mind. The North and the South were fighting. America was split in two.

Patrick enlisted in the army and became bandleader for the 24th Massachusetts Regiment. His music inspired the men in battle and entertained them at camp. The *RUM-TEE-TUM*s that Patrick remembered from his childhood kept the soldiers' spirits high.

But even with music ringing in his ears, Patrick couldn't escape the horrors of war.

When he returned to Boston, Patrick welcomed the troops home. He gave many concerts. But not even the best bands seemed enough to celebrate such a momentous occasion. Patrick found himself wanting to hear *more* notes and *louder* music.

One day, while visiting New York City, Patrick had an idea. It was a big idea. A bold idea. A very, very LOUD idea.

Patrick would create the biggest, boldest, loudest concert the world had ever known. The music would celebrate the bravery of the soldiers! The unity of the land! The end of the war! The concert would be a peace jubilee.

Patrick hurried home and shared his idea with his wife. The celebration would last five days, he said. He would host it in the town he loved: Boston. A huge structure would be built to house the jubilee and the thousands upon thousands of people who would attend—including the president of the United States!

His wife told him he was crazy. She wasn't the only one who thought so.

Everybody said that Patrick's idea was too big. Too bold. And much, much too loud.

People said that the music would sound horrible.

Where was their pomp? thought Patrick. Their pluck? Their love of the world's greatest gift — music?

Patrick refused to listen. "It can be done, and it shall be done!" he exclaimed.

For in his head, he heard a big, bold, and very, very loud melody. It was beautiful.

Patrick told the newspapers all about his big, bold, LOUD idea. Across town, a man named Eben Jordan, who ran a big department store, read about Patrick and his plans. Mr. Jordan admired Patrick's gumption and drive. He decided to raise money to make the jubilee happen.

The starting date for the big event was set: June 15, 1869. Word of the jubilee spread across the country. More than one hundred choruses agreed to sing. Ten times as many musicians said they'd play. From Maine to the Midwest, people began practicing.

With so many visitors bound for Boston, the city pitched in to help. It loaned Patrick a plot of land in the middle of town. Construction for a giant building that Patrick named the Temple of Peace began. Lumber arrived by the foot load. Carpenters came by the trainload. Spectators gathered, too. Many shook their heads. Patrick's plan was simply *too* big.

But three months later, the Temple of Peace was finished. It stood five hundred feet long, three hundred feet wide, and one hundred feet tall. It was covered in 7,500 pounds of paint and braced with ten and a half tons of iron. It had 144 windows and forty-eight toilets.

The Temple of Peace was now the biggest public building in America. It was so big that people were afraid. What if it collapsed? they wondered.

Some days, the talk sent Patrick straight to his bed. Some nights, it kept him wide awake with worry.

But Patrick did what he'd always done: he tuned out the babble—and got even busier.

He rounded up one hundred firemen, one hundred hammers, and one hundred anvils. He gathered a chorus of twenty thousand schoolchildren.

He figured out how to get forty bells to ring

while twelve cannons exploded.

He ordered the creation of the world's largest pipe organ . . .

and a huge bass drum, which traveled across Massachusetts on a flatbed train car to curious crowds.

By the time spring arrived, the whole country was talking about one big, bold, and very, very loud idea: the National Peace Jubilee!

The day before the jubilee was to begin, people poured into Boston from America's tiny towns and big cities. When the hotels filled up, many Bostonians offered to rent rooms in their homes.

Still, people wondered. Would Patrick's music be beautiful? Tomorrow, the world would find out.

On June 15, 1869, Patrick awoke to cloudy skies, followed quickly by a terrible sound:

SPIT - SPAT - SPIT - SPAT - SPIT!

Rain!

Yet the showers couldn't dampen Patrick's spirits. Or the crowds'. People spilled onto the streets. They hung out flags and banners. Booths selling gingerbread, peanuts, and lemonade sprang up around the Temple of Peace. The air smelled of hot coffee.

At three o'clock, one thousand musicians tuned their instruments.
Ten thousand singers took their places beneath two angels holding olive
branches—the sign of peace. The concert was about to start!

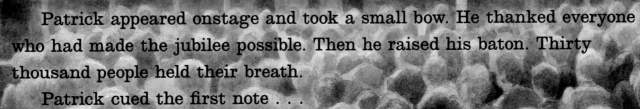

Patrick appeared onstage and took a small bow. He thanked everyone who had made the jubilee possible. Then he raised his baton. Thirty thousand people held their breath.

Patrick cued the first note . . .

and the great jubilee began!

The organ *ROARED!*

The bass drum **THUNDERED!**

The musicians unfurled a GRAND WAVE OF SOUND! It was as LOUD as the ocean! Then as *soft* as a stream. The chorus sang "The Star-Spangled Banner."

The orchestra played church music, then a soaring new song about peace. They even played a march, just like the ones Patrick had loved as a boy. One man dashed from his seat to send his wife a telegram.

COME IMMEDIATELY!
WILL SACRIFICE ANYTHING TO HAVE YOU HERE.
NOTHING LIKE IT IN A LIFETIME!

Next the firemen strutted down the aisles, hammers on their shoulders.

They POUND-POUND-**POUNDED**

their anvils in time to the music.

The cannons **BOOMED!**

The church bells **BONGED!**

DING DONG

DING DONG

The last song? "My Country, 'Tis of Thee." On the final verse, the audience joined in.

As the closing notes hung in the air, the clouds cleared and sunbeams streamed through the 144 windows of the Temple of Peace.

For the next four days, Patrick and his jubilee filled the city with excitement and wonder. On the second day, President Ulysses S. Grant!

On the third day, a solo of fifty trumpets! On the fourth day, an extravaganza for the giant organ! On the fifth and final day, the children's chorus!

When the last note of the last song ended, only one sound rumbled through the Temple of Peace:

Applause!

The audience leaped to their feet!
They whistled. They shouted. They tossed
their hats and waved their handkerchiefs.

CLAP!

CLAP!

CLAP!

CLAP!

CLAP!

CLAP!

CLAP!

Never had they heard anything so big! So bold! So very, very LOUD! And so very, very beautiful.

AUTHOR'S NOTE

A MULTITALENTED MAESTRO

Born in Ballygar, County Galway, Ireland, on Christmas Day, 1829, Patrick S. Gilmore came to America at a time when thousands of Irish people were emigrating to escape poverty and famine. In Boston, his star rose quickly. Besides being an outstanding cornetist, the witty, mustachioed dynamo led the bands that made Boston America's music capital, in particular the Boston Brigade Band and the Salem Brass Band.

One of Gilmore's most lasting contributions was the establishment of an annual Fourth of July concert on the Boston Common—a tradition continued to this day by the Boston Pops on the city's Charles River Esplanade.

Gilmore also composed music. Most famously, his service as regimental bandleader and stretcher bearer in the 24th Massachusetts Regiment during the Civil War inspired him to write and arrange the iconic soldiers' anthem "When Johnny Comes Marching Home."

As for his effect on the troops, one member of the 24th Regiment wrote home, "I don't know what we should have done without our band. It is acknowledged by everyone to be the best in the division. Every night about sundown Gilmore gives us a splendid concert, playing selections from their operas and some very pretty marches, quickstep waltzes, and the like."

A BANNER LINE-UP

Gilmore's first experience organizing a large concert came in 1864. He traveled to New Orleans to oversee the inauguration music for Louisiana's new governor. The extravaganza featured a chorus of 6,000, a band of 500, cannons, and anvils— a taste of what was to come five years later in Boston.

Gilmore began planning the National Peace Jubilee in 1867. In contrast to the torrent of negativity that first greeted the idea, the response to the concert was overwhelmingly positive. Across the country and around the globe, the jubilee was hailed as an artistic and popular success. One newspaper declared it proof that "nothing is impossible."

The City of Boston gave Gilmore $40,000 for his efforts. Although some grumbled about the size of the purse, most felt that it was well earned, as Gilmore nearly went broke organizing the event.